Spider Strike!

T0317891

Contents

Written by Liz Miles

Collins

Lots of spiders spin cobwebs to trap insects.
Then they can bite and eat their **prey**.

Some spiders attack prey with no webs.

This kind of spider leaps.

Spiders are attacked too. They are eaten by lots of animals, such as frogs and lizards.

This book will tell you how spiders attack and how they escape attack!

Cobwebs

Spinning a web:

1 They make a line of silk.

2 They drop, letting Y-shaped lines **stream** out.

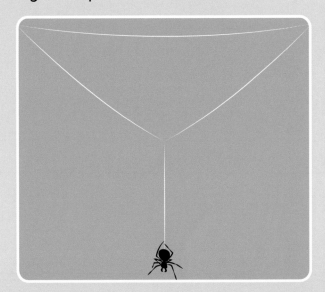

3 They attach each line.

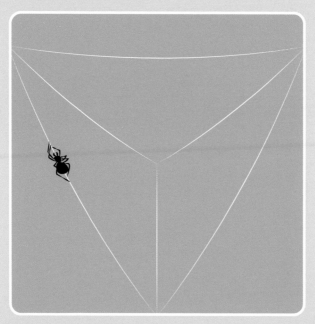

4 They spin a spiral of silk.

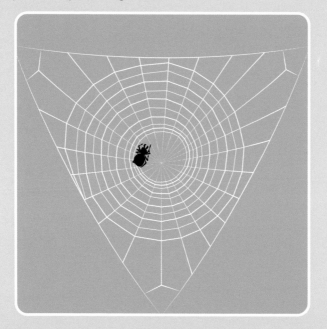

The spider hides until an insect gets stuck.

beads of gum

The spider runs to bite its prey when the web **vibrates**.

Spiders' feet do not stick.

This spider makes a wide net, then drops it on its prey.

A line like a fishing rod streams out of this spider.
If it hits an insect, it sticks!

Some families of spiders make a big web and hide in it.

With this big web, lots of spiders can attack and eat bigger prey.

Weaver spiders hide in pits. If prey steps on
the web, it vibrates and the spider runs to attack.

The weaver spider can then bite its prey to kill it.

Webless attacks

Some spiders do not make webs.

This spider sets a trap. It digs a pit and spins trip-lines.

When prey trips on a line, the spider leaps out.

The **fangs** inject **venom**.

18

This spider's bite can kill.

Spot it by the shape
on its underside.

Jumping spiders leap on prey. To reach it, they need to see well.

This spider attacks its prey by sneaking up and spitting silk with gum and venom.

Staying safe

Spiders stay safe by hiding.

If a spider's leg is grabbed, it might drop off so the spider can escape!

minus one leg

This spider can tip on its side and spin away to reach a hideaway.

You often find spiders hiding under a leaf.

Is this a bud on a twig?

Spiders that help

You do not need to be afraid of all spiders (unless you are an insect!).

Spiders help us a lot. They eat insects that kill our **crops**.

Glossary

crops *food from fields*

fangs sharp teeth

prey animals that are hunted and eaten

stream run out in a long line

venom toxic liquid that can kill an animal

vibrates shakes

Index

Spider parts

Common spider

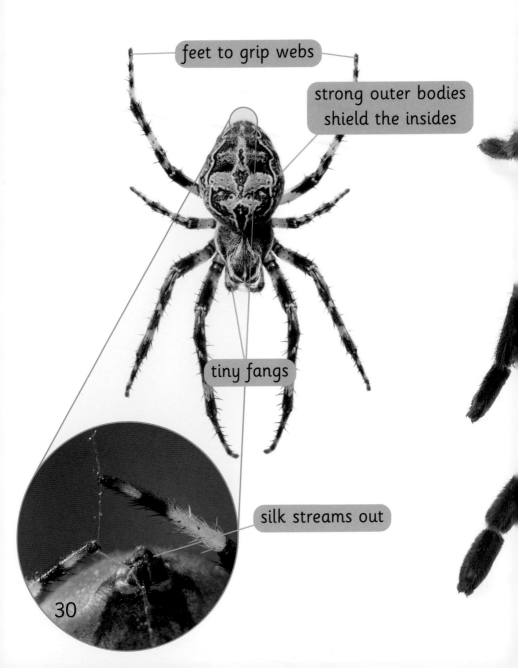

feet to grip webs

strong outer bodies
shield the insides

tiny fangs

silk streams out

30

Goliath spider

good sight

venom sac inside

quick legs

sharp fangs

After reading

Letters and Sounds: Phase 5

Word count: 389

Focus phonemes: /ai/ ay, a-e, ey /ee/ ie, ea /igh/ i-e, i

Common exception words: of, to, the, by, are, be, so, do, when, our, their, no, out, some, you, all, one

Curriculum links: Science: Animals, including humans

National Curriculum learning objectives: Reading/word reading: apply phonic knowledge and skills as the route to decode words; read accurately by blending sounds in unfamiliar words containing GPCs that have been taught; Reading/comprehension (KS2): understand what they read, in books they can read independently, by checking that the text makes sense to them, discussing their understanding and explaining the meaning of words in context; identifying main ideas drawn from more than one paragraph and summarising these

Developing fluency

- Take turns to read a double page, demonstrating how to use expression to make the text interesting and sometimes dramatic.
- Check your child pauses at commas, and notices how this makes the sentences easier to read and understand.

Phonic practice

- Focus on words containing the /igh/ and /ai/ sounds.
  o Turn to page 9 and challenge your child to find words that contain the /igh/ sound. Can they identify the letters that make the /igh/ sound? (*spider*, *bite*, *vibrates*)
  o Turn to page 22 and repeat for words containing /ai/ sounds. (*staying*, *stay*, *safe*)
- Take turns to find words with different /igh/ or /ai/ spellings on other pages.

Extending vocabulary

- Challenge your child to think of as many words as they can to describe the way spiders move. They could begin by thinking of synonyms for:
  page 3: leaps (e.g. *springs*, *bounds*)   page 9: runs (e.g. *races*, *darts*)
  page 21: sneaking (e.g. *creeping*, *prowling*)
  page 24: spin (e.g. *whirl*, *rotate*)